Cello Book

One

by Cassia Harvey

CHP221

6403 N. 6th Street
Philadelphia, PA 19126
www.charveypublications.com

A, B, and C#

Cassia Harvey

The Ladybug: A Hungarian Folk Song

A, B, C♯, and D

Half Notes get 2 counts!

By Our Gates: A Russian Folk Song

Skipping Around the A-String Notes

Contredanse: A Danish Folk Song

Strengthening the 4th Finger

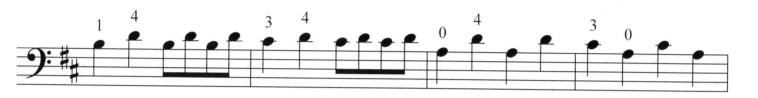

Fiddle Tune

Finger Training on D and A

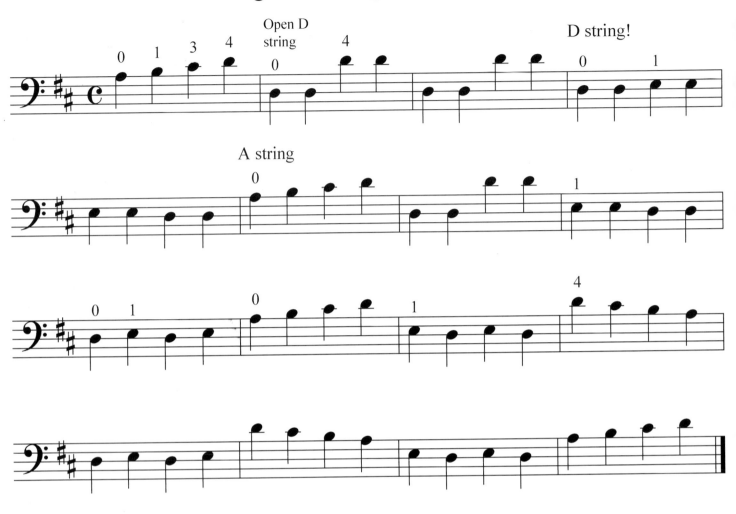

String Crossing

March

Polly Wolly Doodle: An American Folk Song

More notes on the D string

Crossing to the D string

The Bold Soldier: A Traditional Folk Song

Johnny's Gone for a Soldier: An American Folk Song
(play 2 times)

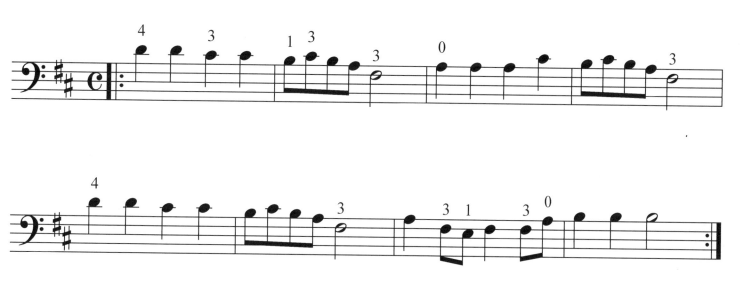

Finger Workout on A and D

Crossing Strings to Third Finger

Jasmine Flower: A Chinese Folk Song

Tibetan Dance

Dotted half notes get 3 counts!

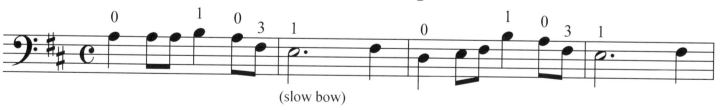

(slow bow)

Crossing Strings to Fourth Finger

More Crossing Strings

Crowninshield's Mother Goose

Crossing Strings and Skipping Notes

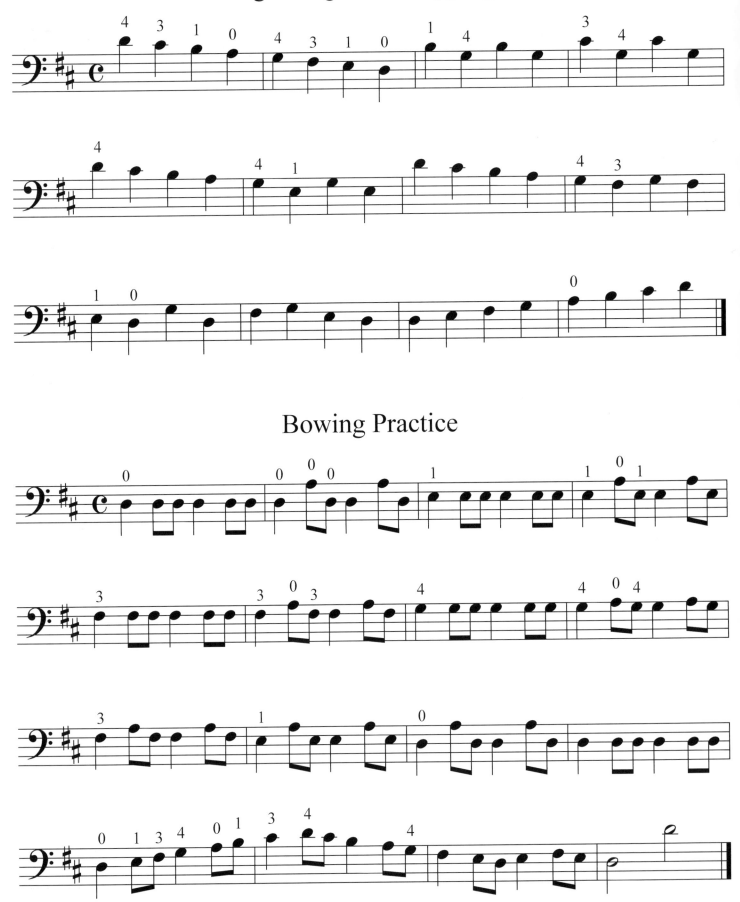

Bowing Practice

Chinese Folk Song

Theme from Schubert's "The Trout"

Exercise to Focus on the D String

Exercise for "Pictures at an Exhibition"

Waltz by Alexandrov

Theme from Mussorgsky's "Pictures at an Exhibition"

Second Finger C♮

Second Finger F♮

Spanish Minuet

Donizetti's Theme from L'Elisir D'Amor

Using 2nd Finger on A and 3rd Finger on D

Third Finger on D: There is an F♯ in the Key Signature!

Third Finger on the G String

Dance from Tchaikovsky's Swan Lake

The Notes on the G string

Crossing Over to the G String

Highland Fiddle Tune

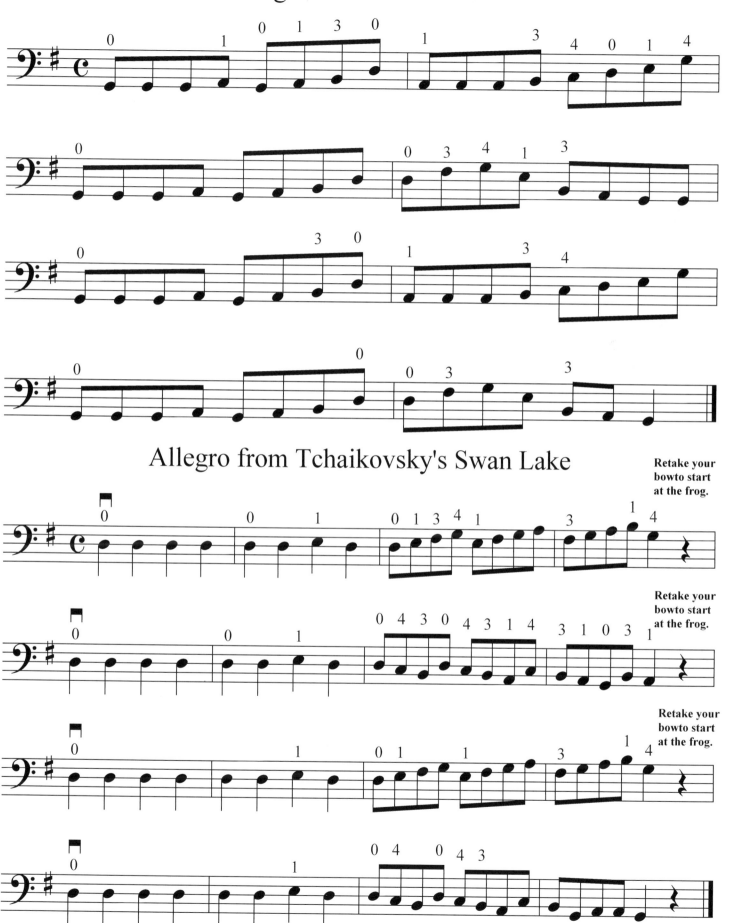

Allegro from Tchaikovsky's Swan Lake

Retake your bow to start at the frog.

Retake your bow to start at the frog.

Retake your bow to start at the frog.

The Notes on the G and C strings

Skipping on G and C

Theme from Rimsky-Korsakov's Scheherazade

Ballet Music from Schubert's Rosamunde

2nd Finger on D and 3rd Finger on G

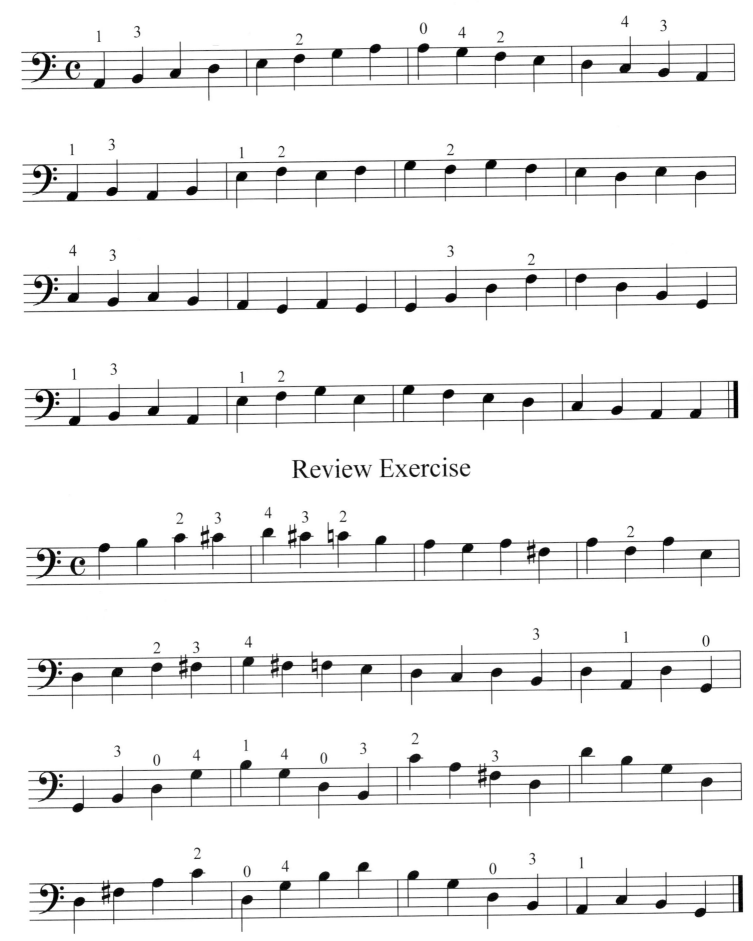

Review Exercise

Theme from Mahler's First Symphony

Galopade, by Glinka

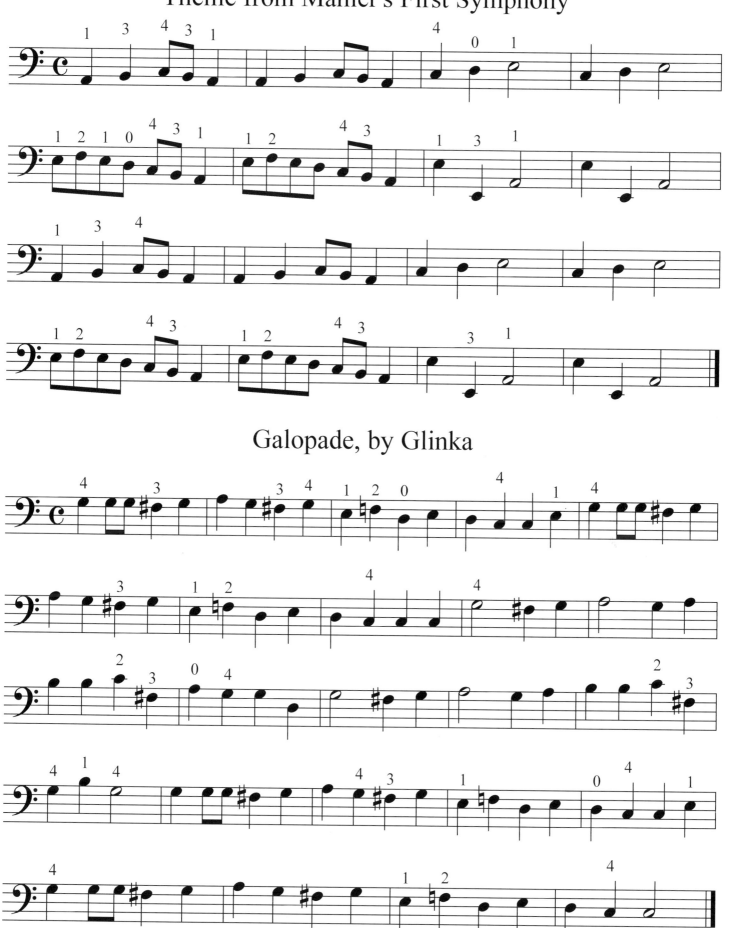

Sliding Back to Low 1st Finger

I Went to Sea for Oranges: A Spanish Folk Song

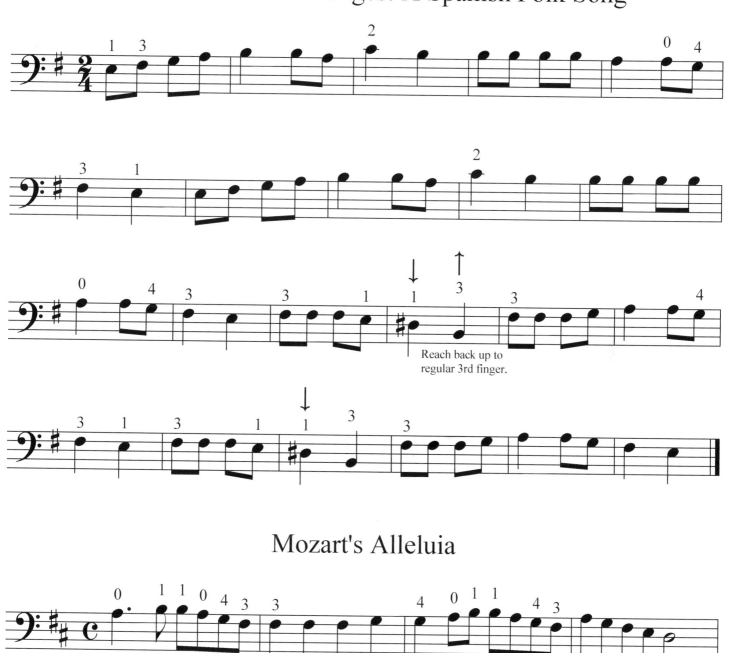

Reach back up to
regular 3rd finger.

Mozart's Alleluia

Reaching Across to High 4th Finger

Sliding to and from High 4th Finger

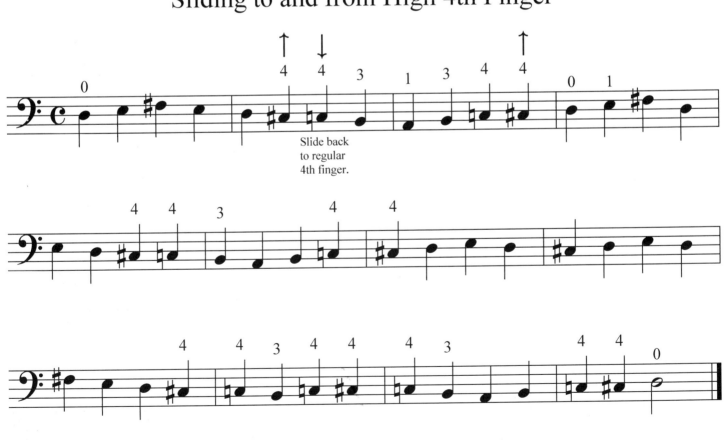

Slide back
to regular
4th finger.

Theme from Beethoven's Symphony No. 6

Cotton-Eyed Joe: A Fiddle Tune

Double Stop Beginnings for the Cello, Book One: CHP220

WEEK 1

Double Stop Exercise 1

Cassia Harvey

Made in the USA
Charleston, SC
11 October 2014